Bigger Problems:

Major Concepts for Understanding Transactions under Islamic law.

Joe Bradford

Copyright © 2019 by Joe W. Bradford, all rights reserved.

This book or any portion thereof may not be reproduced or used in any manner whatsoever without the express written permission of the publisher except for the use of brief quotations in a book review.

Printed in the United States of America

Origem Publishing, First Edition, 2019

Print Edition
ISBN-13: 978-0-9965192-2-9
ISBN-10: 0-9965192-2-X

Bigger Problems:

Major Concepts for Understanding Transactions under Islamic law.

Joe Bradford

CONTENTS

DEFINING CONTRACT 5

FUNCTION OF CONTRACT 9

   Commutative contracts 9

   Donative contracts 10

   Documentary contracts 11

CONDITIONS FOR CONTRACTUAL VALIDITY 13

COMPETENCY AND CAPACITY 15

   Unconscionability 16

OBJECT OF CONTRACT 19

   GHARAR IN CONTRACT 21

   Obscurity (Jahālah) 21

   Non-existence ('Adam) 24

   Inability to deliver ('Ajz 'an al-Taslīm) 25

   The effect of Gharar on Contracts 26

OBLIGATION AND PERFORMANCE 28

   RIBA IN SALES AND DEBTS 29

CONCLUSION 32

INTRODUCTION

بسم الله الرحمن الرحيم

This small text is an abridgement of a longer work I wrote on contracts under Islamic law. Its been my experience that teaching Islamic law many times often than not student get bogged down by the minutia, missing the forest for the trees. The answer has always been "there are bigger problems to worry about, bigger fish to fry." Since "bigger fish" would probably not be the best title for a book on Islamic contracts, I figured I'd stick with the other idiom. The impetus for this text was a challenge: teach a group of 30 students the essentials of contract in 5 hours. The result is this book. Its not meant to be exhaustive. My hope is that it will benefit you and you'll use it as a foundation for further reading and student on this subject.

Joe Bradford

DEFINING CONTRACT

A contract is an enforceable promise. A promise is a commitment to do something you otherwise don't have to do. When you promise someone that you will do something, that means you are obligated to do that thing. The formal promise to do this is a "contract" and the thing you will do is called "performance." The key here is the expectation created by your promise.

When you create a contract freely, you are also creating a set of rights and responsibilities you will be held to. Being "held to" that promise is called enforcement.

You can be held to a promise morally, legally, or both. If you break a promise, you are responsible morally. If you break an unfair contract, you are responsible legally (but maybe not morally). If you break a fair contract, you can be responsible both morally and legally. All contracts are assumed to be valid and permitted until proven otherwise.

FUNCTION OF CONTRACT

Contracts are created to fulfill a certain purpose. This is called its function. If a contract is created for a for-profit exchange, this is called a "commutative" contract. If it is created to gift or give someone something, then is it a "donative" contract. If you simply want to create a record of a right or responsibility, then it is a "documentary" contract.

COMMUTATIVE CONTRACTS are used for transferring property or the use of that property (a right), for providing a service, or creating a partnership. If I sell you something for cash or in installments, I've transferred that property to you. If I leased you an item, I've allowed you to benefit from it in exchange for payment. Same goes for providing a service. If you and I decide to go into business together, we've created a partnership.

DONATIVE CONTRACTS are used for transferring value to another person. They may transfer ownership, like in the case of gifts, awards, bequests, or trusts. They may transfer value without transferring ownership, like cash loans, simple loans (i.e. letting someone borrow something), or indemnity contracts (like guarantees).

DOCUMENTARY CONTRACTS are recording a right or a responsibility. An example of this is a lien (rahn) where I have a right to recuperate something owed to me from another person's property. I've issued a surety (kafala) if I've made a promise to pay or do something on someone else's behalf when they fail to. If I make a deposit with someone, I've simply documented my right left with them for safekeeping, without transferring it to them by sale, gift, or partnership. When I enter into an agreement with someone, I'm simply documenting my intention to perform things mentioned therein.

The rule of thumb here is that it doesn't matter what we call a contract; what matters is how it functions. For example: If someone says, "I gift you this car" and you accept, this is a gift. If someone says, "I gift you this car for 3,000 dollars" and you accept, this is a sale even though you used the word gift.

CONDITIONS FOR VALIDITY

There are seven (7) essential elements that must be present for a contract to be valid: (1) that there be Mutual Assent via offer & acceptance; (2) that there is due consideration for the contract; (3) that the object of contract be known and valid, (4) that the obligation created by the contract be known and valid, (5) that the performance expected from the contract be known and valid; (6) that the parties to the contract meet the standards of legally-defined competency and capacity; and (7) that there be a recognized instrument form.

Each of these seven elements is necessary for a contract to be valid. Depending on which ones are missing, contract may be considered valid or invalid.

COMPETENCY AND CAPACITY

In order to become a party to a contract, you have to be qualified to create one. Competency and capacity are the two things that qualify you to create a contract. To be competent you have to be discerning, able to make your own individual choices and decisions. If you aren't competent, let's say you have some form of short-term memory loss that impairs your decision-making ability, then if you enter into a contract then you (or the other person) have the right to annul or dissolve that contract.

Capacity means that you have the ability to incur legal obligations and acquire legal rights. This excludes people with permanent or chronic mental illnesses or defects, minors, and intoxicated persons. A contract made without capacity is voidable.

UNCONSCIONABILITY

Unconscionability (Zulm) is the act of stipulating terms in your contract that are so unjust that it makes the contract unfair, in a manner that no one with a good conscience would tolerate unless they were forced to. These types of conditions make the contract unenforceable and depending on the situation voidable.

One example of this is misrepresentation. If you were to misrepresent your abilities, the qualities of what you are selling, or your ability to perform, this may make your contract voidable or unenforceable. Other examples are price manipulation, 3rd party counter-offers, and deception.

One exception to this is forcing your partner to sell you their share if they sell it to someone else, called the Right of First Refusal (Shuf'a).

OBJECT OF CONTRACT

The thing that you are selling, leasing, or partnering on etc. is the "object of a contract." It has to be lawful when the contract is made, ascertainable by the time you have to perform what the contracts stipulates, and you have to have the right to exchange this object at the time of contract. In order for something to be "Ascertainable" it has to be free from uncertainty, known as *Gharar*. We'll cover that shortly. Having the right to exchange something means one of two things: you own it outright and can deliver it as described in the contract, or it is fungible, and you are liable for it.

An example of something permitted would be to sell a washing machine, but not a pig. It would be permitted to partner with others to sell washing machines, but not pigs. If you state in your contract that you will sell your friend your washing machine, but you don't own a washing machine, then you've sold something that it is impossible to deliver and can't be identified, which would make your contract void.

GHARAR IN CONTRACT

Uncertainty (Gharar) is caused by three things: obscurity (Jahālah), non-existence ('Adm), inability to deliver ('Ajz 'an al-Taslīm).

OBSCURITY (JAHĀLAH)

Obscurity (Jahālah) is of three types: Excessive, intermediate, and inconsequential.

Excessive Obscurity is when the thing you sell is so obscure that it could be anything of one genus. So if I said: "I sell you an animal," and you say "I'll buy it for money" the object and the value are so broad and obscure that this transaction would be void.

Intermediate obscurity_is when you sell something that is a bit more specific, but still too vague to be meaningful. An example would be: "I offer you a horse for your dollars." Here the genus and class (animal = horse, money = gold) is specified, but not enough to be meaningful.

Negligible Obscurity is any obscurity that remains after this. So, if a person said, "I offer you this horse for 3000 dollars." Not only is this ascertainable, but it's enough information to act on. If a person said, "I'll sell you this Rolex watch for your five 100 dollars bills serial numbers 2354, 2347, 8343, 2097, and 3455." If we leave off the currency's serial numbers, that would be a negligible omission.

NON-EXISTENCE ('ADAM)

Non-existence is exactly what it sounds like. Its inherent to the thing you are selling, causing a level of uncertainty in the contract that it absolute or relative. If I sold you land on the lost continent of Atlantis, that absolutely not exist. If I sold you my neighbor's car, that does exist in an absolute sense, but it doesn't exist as my property relative to what I own. It can also relate to the availability of what's being sold, or how likely it is that the contract can be fulfilled.

INABILITY TO DELIVER ('AJZ 'AN AL-TASLĪM)

Another form of uncertainty is the inability to deliver. This could be actual or constructive. An example of actual inability to deliver would be when I've sold you a car, but it was totaled before I could deliver it. Another example would be me being able to deliver the car, but you are unable to pay for it. Constructive inability implies that the contract cannot, for legal reasons, be completed. An example of this is when you are sold stolen goods or a minor sells you something without the approval of their legal guardian.

THE EFFECT OF GHARAR ON CONTRACTS

Uncertainty affects different contracts differently. In commutative and documentary contracts, if the uncertainty is excessive, it will invalidate the contract. If I offered a non-existent necklace as collateral, that contract would be void.

If the uncertainty is negligible, it will not void the contract. Examples are the possibility that a watermelon is rotten, the possibility that a house's foundation is cracked, or that a business may not profit. Uncertainty has no effect on donative contracts, because there is no value being exchanged.

OBLIGATION AND PERFORMANCE

The obligations that are created by a contract are those duties that each party is legally responsible for in a contract agreement. The obligations created must be permissible in and of themselves, like the object of the contract. As for performance, it may be actual, substantial, partial, or attempted, based on its enforceability. If it is unenforceable, then the performance of the contract or the individual condition is void or voidable.

RIBA IN SALES AND DEBTS

Riba affects commutative contracts. Riba is two types: Sales Riba and Debt Riba.

Sales Riba has two categories: Commodity Riba and Currency Riba. Both are the exchange of unequal amounts of the same counter-value. Examples include: 1 kilo of Basmati rice for 2 kilos of Parboil rice or 1 dollar for 2 dollars, or seven one dollar bills for one ten dollar bill.

If the counter-values are different, the exchange is allowed but there can be no delay in the exchange of the goods (a spot transaction) and each party takes possession of their good immediately. So 1 kilo rice *now* for 2 kilos wheat *now* or 1 USD *now* for 5 pesos *now* then this exchange is valid with the condition it is a spot transaction and possession is taken immediately. If there's a delay in either countervalue or one of them isn't delivered, then the transaction is invalid.

Debt Riba applies to any increase - fixed or floating - on any debt, whether in cash or in-kind, stipulated at the time of contract or at default. Example: I loan you 100 dollars for 120 after 12 months. Or: I sell you a car for 10k due after 12 months, and if you default, I add 30 USD a day until you pay the full amount.

The rule of thumb here is: Every loan that incurs benefit solely to the creditor is considered Riba.

CONCLUSION

This concludes this short text on the major concepts needed to understand transactions and contracts under Islamic law. Its not meant to be an exhaustive work; instead it's for teaching and learning and will hopefully act as a foundation and a stepping stone for students of Islamic law to begin their studies in this important and sometimes harrowing subject.

Joe W Bradford

www.ingramcontent.com/pod-product-compliance
Lightning Source LLC
Chambersburg PA
CBHW070443010526
44118CB00014B/2167